MW01174229

THE
WONDERS
OF PEACE

THE WONDERS OF PEACE

how to see

God's peace at work

in your life

DAVID AYESIYENGA

TATE PUBLISHING
AND ENTERPRISES, LLC

Published by Tate Publishing & Enterprises, LLC
127 E. Trade Center Terrace | Mustang, Oklahoma 73064 USA
1.888.361.9473 | www.tatepublishing.com

Tate Publishing is committed to excellence in the publishing industry. The company reflects the philosophy established by the founders, based on Psalm 68:11,
"The Lord gave the word and great was the company of those who published it."

Book design copyright © 2012 by Tate Publishing, LLC. All rights reserved.
Cover design by Kenna Davis
Interior design by Joel Uber

Published in the United States of America

ISBN: 978-1-61346-971-2
1. Religion; Christian Life, Spiritual Growth
2. Religion; Christian Life, Personal Growth
12.01.25

TABLE OF CONTENTS

INTRODUCTION

Peace is one of the hottest spiritual commodities in our world today. Almost everyone is yearning to enjoy it, but many have gone astray searching for it from the wrong sources. A lot of men are yet to discover its value for a successful walk into the wonders of God.

The concept of peace in the minds of both Christians and non-Christians has to be corrected, because it has been misunderstood and misinterpreted.

It can be looked at in three different ways as: the peace of the world, the peace of God, and peace with men.

THE CONCEPT OF PEACE

THE PEACE OF THE WORLD

Peace I leave with you, My peace I give to you; not as the world do I give to you. Let not your heart be troubled, neither let it be afraid.

John 14:27

In the world, when conditions and situations around a man are good with no trouble, no turmoil, and no confusion, then the person is said to be enjoying peace. This is the peace of the world. Jesus talks about it in John 14:27, but clearly dissociates Himself from it. He mentions the world as the giver of that peace. Everyone in the world is crying for this peace. World leaders are going on meetings in an attempt to instill this peace into the society. Confusion, turmoil, trouble, and war have gripped the society of our day, and the cry of the world is to see peace prevail. However, this kind of peace is temporary and cannot stand the test of time. The reason for that is because it has its source from the world, and whatever is given by men, is not reliable. Jesus, realizing the unreliability of this kind of peace, offers us His peace, a very dependable one. It is this peace that I refer to as the God-kind of peace. It is excellent; and the apostle Paul described it as one surpassing human understanding.

THE GOD-KIND OF PEACE

This is the wonder-working peace and has its source from above. In John.14:27, Jesus was so proud to be associated with it. He ultimately declared Himself as the giver and source of that peace. His name is Wonderful, Counselor, Mighty God, Everlasting Father, and then the prince of peace (Isaiah 9:6)

When He gives you His peace, there is no storm on earth or from Hell that will move you. He has stated clearly in John 14:27 that this is a legacy for His children. It is not for everyone, but for those that belong to the body of Christ. With that peace, you will overcome trouble and fear.

The world is searching for this peace, but through different ways and means. World leaders are searching for it but cannot find it. Peace agreements are signed between nations with the hope of contacting this peace, but it is all an illusion. Many married couples are yearning to enjoy this peace in their matrimonial homes, but it is far from them. The big question is why they are not finding it. It is because they are looking for it in the wrong places. It is with Jesus, the prince of peace, and if we want to enjoy it in our society, marriage, or home, we need to invite Him there. No man can give us any peace as perfect as that given unto us by Jesus. Remember when the apostles let Him into their boat? The winds and storms that rose against them were swallowed right before them. So, if we let Him into our lives, He will give us His peace, and no storm can overcome us in life. Jesus said of Himself: "These things I have spoken to you, that in Me you may have peace…" (John 16:33).

So, it is in Him that we have this peace. We cannot put Him out of our lives and expect to enjoy this peace. David, enjoying this peace, proclaims boldly in Psalm 23:4 that he will fear no evil even in the valley of death. He was not scared about anything, including Goliath, the champion of the Philistines. He declares, "Though an host should encamp against me, my heart shall not fear: though war should rise against me, in this will I be confident," (Psalms 27:3).

Such bold confession and declaration can only come from a man walking in the peace of God. The apostle Paul walked in this peace too and described it as one surpassing

how to see God's peace at work in your life

all understanding. It surpasses all understanding, because when you have it, you will be smiling at the storms and winds that rise against you. When there is a casting down, then will you be seeing a rising-up.

Get connected to it, and it will help you overcome the troubles and storms that rise against you. It is indeed a wonder!

It Is a Wonder

Anything which cannot be explained in the human context is a wonder. A wonder cannot be understood, and the peace of God is a wonder, because it surpasses all understanding. It is a wonder and a pacesetter for many other wonders. Paul enjoyed it. He treasured it, and had this to say about it: "...and the peace of God which surpasses all understanding shall keep your hearts and minds through Christ Jesus" (Phil 4:7).

Observe the way Paul describes it. Look at the value he attaches to it. He commands the Philippians to let it be a valuable treasure in their hearts, because it will keep their minds and hearts in Christ. Therefore, it is impossible for a man to have his way out of Christ with this peace in his life.

I realized personally that anytime Satan wants to launch his weapons against humanity, the first thing he tries to steal is the peace of God. When he succeeds, then he proceeds. He has succeeded in putting asunder marriages, families, churches, and organizations through this strategy. The couple of a family must beware of this, and give the devil no place. The pastor of a church in the moments of a church crisis should stop pointing accusing fingers at the leaders and members, and call upon God for His peace to reign.

The peace of God has what it takes to overcome and swallow troubles, and that is why Paul describes it as surpassing all understanding. Get connected to it, and your life will see color, and beauty. Your broken home, marriage, church, or organization will receive another touch of the Lord.

how to see God's peace at work in your life

PEACE WITH MEN

Therefore, if you are offering your gift at the altar,
then remember that your brother has something
against you; leave your gift there in front of the altar.
First go and make peace to your brother and then
come and offer your gift.

Matthew 5:23

We cannot claim to have a good relationship with God and
not have one with the men we live with. That is hypocrisy,
and the Lord will not accept our gift when we refuse to
obey the promptings of the Holy Spirit to make peace with
men who may have something against us.

We are in the days that people come to the altar of
the Lord with gifts without listening to any promptings
from the Spirit of God. There are many people today in
the kingdom of God seeking for the blessing of worship

without any regard for peace with men. Jesus is saying that peace must precede worship, otherwise you have nothing to gain. He stated that blessed are the peace-makers, they shall be called Sons of God (Matthew 5:9). A child of God should be a peace-loving person, and seek to be at peace with men. "Depart from evil, and do good. Seek peace and pursue it" (Psalms 34:14).

Therefore, it is required of us to put away bitterness, and make peace with men. We cannot succeed in our worship to God with our hearts filled with pain and bitterness against our neighbor. God will not accept anything we offer Him in that state.

Sometimes, you see believers gather to pray to God on an issue, but many may have their hearts filled with anxiety, pain, and bitterness. A prayer topic is raised, and everyone bursts into tongues, believing God to perform wonders. Sadly, they finish the meeting but do not see God move. They get disappointed, wondering what probably went wrong. Nothing actually went wrong, but the altar of peace in the hearts of the people was not in place. So, all the tongues that were spoken in the meeting had no basis.

God is not dead. He is still on the throne and ready to hear you. All you need to do is to put the foundation of peace right, before moving on to other things, and He will smile at you. You might wonder why a marriage will be tearing apart, and all cries to God for His intervention has failed. It is because peace has departed from that home, and

Satan has moved in. Remember, any time the peace of God moves out, Satan moves in.

Some believers are the first to stir up trouble, and the first to cry to God for His intervention. Stop stirring the trouble, and let the peace of God reign in that family, marriage, or church, and you will experience His amazing wonders.

I have seen churches where confusion carries the order of the day. The pastor and deacons are in a scuffle, and the members are at serious loggerheads. In such churches, the peace of God has left, and Satan has taken charge. God is simply out of such churches, and His wonders are temporarily suspended until peace is restored. Keep away from such places until peace is restored. It is for your own safety, because you could be a causality of war and not a candidate for wonders.

I know the story about a church that was not experiencing growth for many years all because of a long standing dispute between the worship leader and another leader of that church. Many evangelism steps taken for the church to grow failed, and nobody understood what was happening. But one night, the dispute was resolved, and then the worship leader, with a trembling voice, took all the blame, apologized to the church, and asked for forgiveness from the church and from the other leader. From that day, the veil of darkness that was over the church was lifted, and a new light dawned on it. Shortly after that, the church experienced a tremendous growth. And that is the wonders peace can do.

In another instance, a couple was married for many years without the fruit of the womb. They had been to the best hospitals for check-ups, but the results proved they had no problem of infertility. Next, they moved from one pastor to the other for prayers, but they got no results.

Then they opted to seek counseling on the issue, and guess what happened.

It came to light during the counseling session that the woman was not happy in the marriage. Tension had been created in the home, because of the behavior of the man. He came home moody, behaving as if the woman he once loved had become a monster. The joy they once shared in their marriage was gone, and this time the communication lines in the marriage were cut off.

The man was advised to go home, make peace with the wife, and come back in three months time for further counseling.

He obeyed, and the next time he appeared, he was having a song in his mouth. Praise to the name of the Lord! The woman who had been barren for years now picked a seed. It worked for him and can also do the wonders for you too in your marriage. Stop crying and wishing for a change of a life partner, you did not make a mistake. Both of you were meant to be together before the foundations of the earth. Stop cursing your partner, and the children the Lord blessed you with. Stop speaking negative words into their lives. They are God's gifts and must be treated with care.

how to see God's peace at work in your life

Peace for Answered Prayers

> But now, the lord, my God had given me rest on every side, so that there is neither adversary nor evil concurrent.
>
> 1 Kings 5:4

This was King Solomon testifying about the rest God had given him. He was the only king of Israel who never went to war during his reign. What was the secret?

Think about it! It is a real wonder, but it's true. Israel experienced no war when Solomon was in the helm of affairs. There was no war or evil occurrence during his reign.

Solomon means *peace*, and by the time peace reigned in the affairs of Israel, all the wars and evil occurrences ceased. Allow the peace of God to rule in your life, and the battles of your life will be over. Beware that any time the peace of God reigns in your life, there is no war that you cannot conquer, and no evil will come near thy dwelling place.

The peace of God is a pacesetter to answered prayers. Israel prayers for conquest over the enemy came in force as soon as they had a Solomon. First, get the peace of God into your life, and it will pave a way for answers to your prayers.

> Be careful for nothing, but in everything, by prayer and supplication with thanksgiving, let your requests be known unto God: And the peace of God, which surpasseth all understanding shall keep your hearts and minds through Christ Jesus.
>
> Philippians 4:6-7

When a man's heart is devoid of the peace of God, his request to God is hindered, and he obtains little or no results in prayer. That is why it is not good to go before God with bitterness, anxiety, pain, or worry in your heart. Anyone with all these unwanted elements in his heart is walking in iniquity, and God will not answer prayers from his lips.

> Behold, the Lord's hand is not shortened that it cannot save; neither is his ear heavy, that he cannot hear. But your iniquities have separated between you and your God, and your sins have hid his face

> from you, that He will not hear. For your hands are defiled with blood, and your fingers with iniquity; your lips have spoken lies, your tongue had muttered perverseness.
>
> Isaiah 59:1-3

What is God saying here? His word to you is that a prayer from a heavy heart is perverse before Him. He is hearing nothing good from your tongue but perverseness, and such prayers, He will not accept.

I have been to prayer meetings where people offered only complaints to God, and thought they were praying. They made a chain of complaints to God from a heart so bitter, and yet expected the Lord God to be there. He will not be there. Remember, He is enthroned in the praises of His people, not in their complaints. He will hear requests from a heart of peace, not a complaining heart. Complaining breeds anxiety and steals away the peace of God in a man's life.

ANXIETY IS A KILLER

Anxiety is a killer of the peace of God. So run away from it! It hinders a man from tapping into the wonders of God through prayer.

Hannah's prayers for a baby year after year were without answers because of anxiety.

how to see God's peace at work in your life

> And her adversary also provoked her sore, for to make her fret, because the Lord had shut up her womb. And as she did so year by year, she went up to the house of the Lord, so she provoked her; therefore she wept.
>
> 1Samuel 1:6-7

Provocation from her rival made Hannah anxious and bitter. And for many years, the miracle for a baby was delayed until she learned to walk in the peace of God.

> Then Eli answered and said, Go in peace, and the God of Israel grant thee thy petition that thou has asked of him.
>
> 1Samuel 1:17

So, walking in the peace of God gives Him the chance to step into our lives with answers to our prayers.

One time, David nearly slipped out of the will of God because of his anxiety to prosper like the wicked.

> But as for me, my feet were almost gone; my steps had well nigh slipped. For I was envious at the foolish, when I saw the prosperity of the wicked…when I thought to know this, it was too painful for me.

how to see God's peace at work in your life

Until I went into the sanctuary of God, then understood their end.

Ps.73:2, 3, 16, 17

Envy of others and the prosperity of the wicked can be the cause of anxiety. It creates pain in a person's heart and takes him or her out of the will of God. David was in pain and got envious of the prosperity of the wicked. He admitted that he almost lost focus and direction in God because of envy. His trouble started when he envied the prosperity of the wicked. Envy brings anxiety to a man, so drive it far away from your heart. Remember, you were created to live an enviable life, not to envy others, and you need to walk with that understanding in your spirit mind.

David compared himself to the wicked and wondered where the power of his God was. That was his mistake. We were not born to compare ourselves with other people but to manifest the glory of God. Creation, and the wicked are in earnest expectation for our manifestation, so why now compare ourselves to the wicked? Stop comparing yourself to others, and serve your God with joy, for "godliness with contentment is great gain," (1Tim 6:6).

I know believers who got into trouble and desperately called on God for His intervention, and when nothing happened, they abandoned Him for the devil, claiming He had not been fair to them. Serve your God in peace, and

how to see God's peace at work in your life

He will prove Himself on your behalf. Allow God to vindicate you, and you will have a story to tell someday.

The wisest man, Solomon, made this observation about anxiety: "Anxiety in the heart of man causes depression…" Proverbs 12:25a.

Anxiety has sent many lives to the bed of depression. It has stolen peace from the hearts of many lives and ruined them completely. It must not be entertained! Run away from it, and you will enjoy the wonders of God. Another killer of the peace of God is a wavering heart.

A Wavering Heart

A wavering heart is a heart full of doubt. It is a heart that cannot be steadfast on God. People with a wavering heart cannot wholly trust God for their needs. They have one eye on the Lord and the other eye elsewhere. They have a part of their heart for the Lord and the other part in something else. People with such an attitude end up receiving nothing from the Lord in prayer.

> But let him ask in faith, nothing wavering. For he that wavereth is like a wave of the sea driven with the wind and tossed. For let not that man think that he shall receive anything from the Lord. A double-minded man is unstable in all his ways.
>
> James 1:6-8

Wavering steals the peace of God from a man. It hinders God from reaching out to him. Remember God is not interested in an unstable mind, and we need to trust Him for everything. He requires of us to meditate on His word and walk in it daily. He expects us to trust His word, taking hold of all the promises thereof. He does not expect us to doubt Him. Doubt and fear cause double-mindedness and hinder us from experiencing the wonders of God.

Abraham could not trust God for a child, and was so scared he would die childless, but little did he know that God had many descendants in store for him. Never doubt God on what He can do.

He is able to do things beyond our imagination. Sometimes, some Christians cannot trust God for marriage partners in the Lord, and so abandon God, and the Church for unbelievers. Many who do this will tell you they are getting old, and cannot wait any longer. After all, they can marry an unbeliever, and convert him to the Lord. But clearly, this is a lie from the pit of hell. Where on earth has clean water ever overpower unclean water when mixed together? It is the opposite.

Friend, in all your ways, always wait for God to come. His time is the best, and not our time. If we go ahead of Him through any foul or fair means, we will crash badly with no one to rescue us.

how to see God's peace at work in your life

PEACE IN MARRIAGE

Even as Sarah obeyed Abraham, calling him lord whose daughter ye are, as long as ye do well, and are not afraid with any amazement.

Likewise, ye husbands, dwell with them according to knowledge, giving honor unto the wife as unto a weaker vessel, and as being heirs together of the grace of life; that your prayers be not hindered.

1 Peter 3:6-7

This scripture above unfolds the secret to answered prayers in marriage. I believe by now you are beginning to see that not all the problems in marriage are from the devil. Sometimes, it does not require any binding and losing of the devil for a marriage to work. It only takes the peace of God in that marriage to make a difference. The woman ought to live with the man with humility and honor .The man must live with the woman according \to knowledge, understanding clearly that she is a weaker vessel. Seek knowledge through books on marriage, through marriage seminars, through counseling from successful and experienced marriage counselors or couples and through the word of God. Apply it to bring peace into your marriage, and you will experience great wonders in that marriage. When peace reigns in your home, you will receive answers from heaven to your prayers; otherwise, you will shed all the tears on earth with no answer from God.

> And this have ye done again, covering the altar of the Lord with tears, with weeping, and with crying out, insomuch that he regarded not the offering any more, or receiveth it with good will at your hand. Yet ye say, wherefore? Because the Lord hath been witness between thee and the wife of thy youth, against whom thou has dealt treacherously, yet is she thy companion, and the wife of thy covenant.
>
> Malachi 2:13-14

In the days of Malachi, certain husbands went before the altar of God weeping because the Lord would not accept their act of worship and offering. They kept wondering what the problem was. Then God sent the prophet Malachi to warn them about the manner in which they dealt treacherously with the wives of their youth. The Lord went on to explain that such an act was a violation of the marriage covenant of which He has been a witness. Therefore, He closed His ears to their prayers and would not accept offerings from them.

Friend, be careful that you do not go before God to make vows you don't mean. There are serious implications for breaking such vows, and God will not suffer you to go free. God Himself will fight you anytime you break the vows, and that is why married couples should be careful the way they handle each other. You don't make a promise before God and a crowd of witnesses to love and cherish your partner but then deal treacherously with that partner afterwards. It is a violation of the marriage covenant and can be the reason why the Lord will not answer your prayers. When the Lord closes His ears to our prayers, we don't get it as the Lord in action for violation of our marriage covenant; instead we tend to heap blame on our partner or the devil for our marriage woes. As much as it is true that marriage is among Satan's top destructive targets, I think that if married couples handle each other with love and care in accordance with their marriage vows, he will have no place in the marriage. I know women who got into good marriages, but started experiencing problems after a while. They moved from one prayer meeting to the other crying to God for His intervention, but He will not hear them. They tended to wonder why, but failed to realize they did not live up to the vows they took before God.

Married couples supposedly make vows during weddings to have and hold their partner "from that day forward; for better for worse, for richer for poorer, in sickness and in health, to love and cherish, till death us do part, according to God's holy ordinance." However, some throw away or forget the words of their marriage vows after the wedding ceremony and then do it their way. That is a violation of God's covenant. We must not take the words of a marriage vow as ordinary words. They must not be seen or treated as anything light either. Those words are very important for success in a marriage. If married couples can live by their marriage vows, they will enjoy the best of God's blessing in that marriage. If married couples could work out their marriage in a manner that reflects the very words they recited before God during their wedding ceremony, they will enjoy great peace and receive answers to prayers they make to the Lord.

I know some men who took women to the altar and afterwards started dating other women. When their wives attempted to stop such immoral acts, they received the worst treatment from them. So, the wives held their peace and kept sobbing each night. As the unfaithful husbands continued their evil, God rose up against them. Some got involved in car accidents and repented, but it was too late. Others were caught in broad day light adultery, beaten up, and humiliated. For others, they lost big businesses and contracts, and that brought them home.

Husbands should love their wives as Christ loved the church, but this does not mean the wife should abuse such love. I have seen loving husbands, including pastors, who are under bondage in the hands of their wives and wished they were out of the union. Marriage is supposed to make life better and not worsen the life of any partner, and nobody should take advantage of marriage vows to mistreat or manipulate his or her marriage partner. My point here is that certain married people will fail to live up to their obligations and expectation in a marriage. They will mistreat and manipulate their partners because they believe that their partner will be there for them till death **separates** them. Although that is right, you should not make life unbearable for your partner. If the heat is **too** much, he or she might jump out of the marriage in disobedience to the commandments and ordinance of God. This is not good or profitable to either partner.

Having the peace of God in your life also paves a way for angelic ministration.

how to see God's peace at work in your life

Peace for Angelic Ministration

Many times I have come across believers who just wished they could have an angelic encounter. Some doubting folks in the Lord have also questioned me about the existence of angels, and others wanted to know how best they could have a personal encounter with angels.

These questions moved me to study deep into the Bible on the subject of angels. It took me to Jesus, and His earthly ministry, and then to Daniel, Elijah, Peter, Paul, and the many others you can think of.

In my study, I noticed that Jesus enjoyed much angelic ministration while on earth. In fact, angels were His personal aid. He never called for them, yet they were always around to minister to Him whenever it was necessary. They were His friends, and He did not need any special prayer before they could come around. He did not need any fasting and prayer or all-night prayer before they appeared. It is recorded of Him in the Bible that He had the power to call more than twelve legions of angels instantly (Matt 26:5).

Angels were so real to Jesus right from birth until His death, and that amazed me so much. From then onwards, I began wondering why a man enjoyed such an avalanche of angelic encounters, and yet in our day, it's rare to have one such encounter. Was it because He was the Son of God? The answer is a big *no*. It is all because Jesus is the prince of peace. It was the peace of God all over Him that attracted the angels to him and paved the way for such terrific angelic ministration.

Peace is a pacesetter for angelic ministration, and once it gets settled in your life, you become a candidate for angelic encounters. I noticed that Jesus Christ enjoyed angelic ministration all His life on earth except on the cross. Remember, the only time that God forsook His Son was on the cross. What happened, and why did He not get angelic attention this time?

It was on the cross that Jesus got embittered. He had been inflicted with a nail. A crown of thorns was put on Him, with the sins of the world on Him. Isaiah 53:4-5 clearly states that he was bruised, borne our grieves and sorrows, and the chastisement of our peace was upon him. As a result, He cried to His God but got no answer.

how to see God's peace at work in your life

And at the ninth hour, Jesus cried with a loud voice, saying E'loi E'loi la'ma Sabach'tha-ni? Which is being interpreted. My God, My God, why have you forsaken me.

Mark 15:34

Is that not unbelievable? It is the first time in the Bible that Jesus cried out to the Father, and yet received no angelic attention. Why was it so? Why was He forsaken by the Almighty God this time? Where were the many angels that used to attend to Him? Why were they not doing it this time around? Your guess can be as good as mine. The prince of peace had become the prince of iniquities having all the iniquities of the world on Him. The peace in Him was gone, and as a result, almighty God could not look in His direction let alone send an angel to attend to Him.

Friend, any time the peace of God departs from your life, it makes it hard for you to receive angelic ministration. Peace is what sets the pace for angelic ministration, so get rid of all the filthy garments around you, so that the angels can reach out to you.

REMOVE THE FILTHY GARMENTS

Filthy garments are things in our lives that hinder God from reaching out to us. They are things that steal away the peace of God. To some, it is worry, and the cares of the world, and to others, it is anxiety, pain, and agony. There are people who can agonize over an issue in their heart for years and will not let it go. Such an issue becomes a filthy garment to their heart. Others have nursed pain for years and will not let it go, and this too is a filthy garment to the heart.

How will the angels reach out to you? Think about it, and take a survey of your life one more time. Allow all the filthy garments in your heart to go. It will pave the way for angelic ministration, and the wonders of God will be real to you.

> And he showed me Joshua, the high priest, standing before the Angel of the Lord, and Satan standing at his right hand to resist him. And the Lord said unto Satan, the Lord rebuke thee Satan, even the Lord that had chosen Jerusalem rebuke thee: is not this a brand plucked out of fire? And Joshua was clothed with filthy garments, and stood before the Angel. And he answered and spake unto those that stood before him, saying, Take away the filthy garments from him. And unto him he said, Behold, I have caused thine iniquity to pass from thee, and I will clothe thee with change of garment.
>
> Zechariah 3:1-4

Friend, you need a change of garment to pave a way for angelic ministration. Joshua's story says it all. An angel was there to minister to him but was hindered by a filthy garment. That filthy garment attracted Satan to the scene to resist Joshua.

I remember Jesus saying that He saw the devil coming to Him, but then nothing of his was found in Him. Satan had no filthy garment in Christ, and no wonder the Lord Jesus could bind him easily. You are binding and losing the devil, and nothing is happening because of his filthy garment in you. Give it up, and the devil will respect your command from today.

Joshua was so close to the angel, yet *far* from him, because the angel could not minister to him. As believers, we must not allow filthy garments to hinder our lives. We have to let the filthy garments go, and we will experience something different about God.

Though Joshua was a high priest; he had a filthy garment. So, you could have a filthy garment in you no matter the kind of title you hold in the church or society. He could have remained in that state had the almighty God not intervened. Don't pretend about it. Check your life, and do a good job for yourself. God will not come down to remove them for you. You are the one required to give up those filthy garments.

In 1998, I was leading a prayer meeting in Kintampo in the Brong-Ahafo region of Ghana. There was a lady who came to the meeting with a bitter heart expecting healing of a prolonged ailment that modern medicine and the prayers

how to see God's peace at work in your life

of great pastors had failed to handle. I was ministering to some people in that meeting, and then at some point in the meeting, the Lord whispered to me about this lady. It was about her bitter heart. She had been bitter with her sister-in-law trying to interfere into her marriage. When I received this word from the Lord, I stopped everything I was doing and headed in her direction.

Then the Lord continued, "I am ready to heal her, but she must let go that garment of bitterness in order to receive the healing."

I announced it, and she acted accordingly. Friend, the next thing I saw was a flashing glory from heaven over her head, and this occurred within the twinkle of an eye. I declared loudly what I had seen, and behold, that was the end of that sickness. The lady was set free instantly.

Many people like this woman are wondering why God will not heal them of certain ailments after many years of prayers. Many serving God today are wondering why they are hindered from receiving the blessings of God. Some have prayed for years to the Lord without answers to their prayers and are left with a lot of doubt and questions about God. But the bottom line is that a filthy garment in a man's life must be given up in order for the glory of God to be seen.

Another way to pave the way for angelic ministration is to put to rest all the issues causing the filthy garments, and allow God to reign.

Put Issues to Rest

Do you want to pave the way for angelic ministration in the worst issues of your life? Then put those issues to rest, and meet God with a cheerful heart.

> But he himself went a day's journey into the wilderness, and came and sat down under a juniper tree, and he requested for himself that he might die, and said, it is enough; now, O lord, take away my life: for I am not better than my fathers. And as he lay and slept under a juniper tree, behold, then an angel touched him, and said Arise and eat.
>
> 1Kings 19:4-5

There were worrying issues in Elijah's life. He got to a point that he put off his servant and wished he was dead. He sat under a Juniper tree crying and declaring that he had come to the end of the road. To him, he had enough troubles, and life was not worth living again. The peace in his heart was gone. The heart which once poured out praises to God was now full of complaints. It's clear from the scripture above that nothing could convince Elijah to put to rest the worries of his life. He had written his death warrant, and all He wanted was a signature of the Lord for his exit from the earth.

how to see God's peace at work in your life

God had sent an angel to intervene in Elijah's situation, but he could not be reached with the blessings. An *issue* had to be put to rest to pave the way. The Bible records that as soon as Elijah slept, behold, an angel touched him. I believe the angel was right there, but could not touch him because the *issues* were not put to rest yet. Note the word *behold*, and see how the touch was so fast and easy. Until you put to rest those worrying issues in your life, and give peace a chance, you will not enjoy angelic ministration. The fact that you are facing many challenges does not mean God cannot do something about it. Remember, He is the omnipotent Jehovah and has the whole world in His hands. If He can make rivers even in the wilderness, why will you think He cannot meet your need?

The account on Elijah suggests to me that in our worries, challenges, and troubles, the Lord God sends an angel to minister to us, but we are sometimes denied such ministration because we hold so tight to the issues instead of holding fast to the Lord. David always looked up to the Lord instead of the worrying issues, and God became his present help in trouble (Psalms 46:1).

Some people often think God does not care when they are in their moments of trouble. They forget that He is a loving God and has compassion on us comparable to that which a mother has for her child. Brethren, look up to God, and put those worrying issues to rest. It will pave a way for God to step into your situation.

And when Herod would have brought him forth, the same night he was sleeping between two soldiers, bound with two chains; and the keepers before the door kept the prison. And behold, the angel of the lord came upon him, and a light shined in the prison; and he smote Peter on the side, and raised him up, saying, Arise up quickly. And the chains fell off from his hands.

Acts 12:6-7

What a peace in a man's heart! The night before Peter would be brought forth before Herod, he did not lose any sleep worrying over the death trial before him. Thank God for men like him. They make Christianity simple and beautiful. Peter cared not about the death issue before him knowing that God is the only deliverer at that point. Remember, if God cannot deliver you out of that which seems insurmountable, no man or demon can. It is as simple as that, and you need to walk with this revelation in mind.

I am not surprised an angel appeared right on time to rescue Peter. I call this angelic timing. Start walking in the peace of God, and you will enjoy angelic timing also. The angels will always be right there on time for you.

I know children of God who in moments of trouble behave as if God neither exists nor has the power to save. They cry and worry over every little issue. They forget that God is almighty and can make a way even when there

how to see God's peace at work in your life

43

seems to be no way. Pray and relax, for your case is not bigger than Peter's. It's not too big for God. Give peace a chance, and God will be there on time for you.

Personally, I have had angelic encounters at times that I was very relaxed and put to rest the *issues* of my life. One time, I was praying for direction in one area of my ministry. I made time with God, fasting and praying, but got no word from Him. I was getting frustrated over the issue, and the more I prayed, the more I became frustrated. Oh mine! I just needed a word from the Lord to make a major decision, but received nothing. After sometime, I decided to put the issue to rest, and allow my mind to rest. Thus, the matter was temporarily suspended, and peace took over.

Some months later, I was relaxing my mind at a guest house, and this time I was not engaged in any spiritual activity. Then, suddenly an angel descended into my room, touched me, and brought me a message from God on what I had prayed earlier on .It was so real that I cannot forget the experience.

Put to rest those things that bring worries to your life, and watch what the Lord will do. I have experienced it, and I know that it works and will work for you.

Peace in the life of a man also paves a way for divine intervention.

PEACE FOR DIVINE INTERVENTION

In life we sometimes encounter issues that appear to be beyond our control. In such moments, all we need is the Lord's intervention. There is a way everybody handles such issues, but the most obvious and common choice for most people is prayer and fasting. You appear a lunatic to men if all you do is to praise God for that *unconquerable* problem. People expect you to break down in worry, anxiety, and make complaints to God. I have seen people who in times of crisis started blaming God for not intervening before the problem arrived. They castigate Him, and cite examples of others who never served Him, yet are without such problems. They get bitter with God, and prayer from their hearts is nothing but complaints.

Friend, it does not work that way. God will not move for you in your bitter state. He will show Himself strong to people with a cheerful heart. These are the people who praise Him even under the worst conditions of life. They don't know defeat. A thankful heart creates a thankful home. With a thankful heart in your life, God will make your life His home, and all the problems will get lost.

The peace of God is thus the pacesetter for divine intervention. God desires prayers and supplications from a heart full of thanksgiving. Remember, He inhabits the praises of His people, not their complaints.

Stop crying to Him with bitterness in your heart. Allow peace to reign in your heart, and He will intervene on your behalf. He has done it for others and will do it for you too.

> And the multitude rose up together against them: and the magistrates rent their clothes, and commanded them to beat them. And when they had laid many stripes upon them, they cast them into prison, charging the jailor to keep them safely. Who having received such a charge, thrust them into the inner prison, and made their feet fast in the stocks. And at mid night, Paul and Silas prayed, and sang praises unto God: and the prisoners heard them. And suddenly there was a great earthquake, so the foundations of the prison were shaken: and immediately all the doors were opened, and every one's band were loosed.

Acts 16:22-26

What an excellent deliverance! This was a deliverance which did not take prayer and fasting. It did not take any binding and losing of the devil. It was not an earthly judicial vindication. All it took for such a mighty intervention from the almighty God was a prayer from a cheerful heart. This was all God needed for an intervention. A cheerful heart is a peaceful heart, and peace in the life of a man paves the way for a divine intervention. The judicial council of heaven will rule in your favor against unconquerable situations when you call unto God with a cheerful heart.

Thank God for the lives of Paul and Silas. They sang praises aloud to the hearing of their prison inmates when they were supposed to be remorsed, disappointed, and rejected. They blessed God for the situation, and then cried to Him for intervention. From today, if you will learn to bless God for every situation before crying to Him, you will see His intervention. Being still also set the pace for divine intervention.

BEING STILL

The expression being still could be interpreted in many different ways. It means to look up to God in the face of affliction. It is looking up to the Lord as your first and last solution amidst any affliction or problem.

When you are still in tough times, it is an indication of a high level of trust in God. He is then left with no option but to act on your behalf. Friend, God is a God who weighs the actions and thoughts of men and he knows it when you are still. He commands us to be still in the turbulent stages of our life. Be still in the fires, in the stormy winds, and in the troubled waters; it will cause the Lord to intervene in your situation. There is certainly a connection between being still and divine intervention.

> Be still, and know that I am God: I will be exalted among the heathen, I will be exalted in the earth.
>
> Psalms 46:10

David is giving us a secret. That secret is being still in the face of challenges. It is having the peace of God in your troubled moments of life. He is saying that peace is a pacesetter for divine intervention. He was a mighty warrior, and this was his secret. No enemy could frighten him, not even Goliath, the champion of the Philistines. He won battles with this secret and became great and famous. God becomes God when you are still .He proves to the world that He is alive for you. He does wonders that beat your understanding.

The peace of God is a key to divine intervention. Grab it, adore it, and you will win your battles. Some people run everywhere when trouble looms. They forget there is a God who reigns in the affairs of men and holds the deep places of this earth in His hands. There is nothing too hard for Him, for He is the Lord God of all flesh. He is bigger than sickness, death, barrenness, financial crisis, failure, disappointment, cancer, etc.

All He wants from you is to be still, look up to Him, and then He will show Himself as God. He is a God with a divine hand that is not short to save. In His dealings with Israel, He commanded them to be still if they desired to see divine victories.

> And Moses said unto the people, Fear not, stand still, and see the salvation of the lord, which he will show you today: for the Egyptians whom you have seen today, ye shall see them again no more forever. The lord shall fight for you, and ye shall hold your peace.
>
> Exo.14:13-14

God commanded them to fear not, and to remain still in order to see His salvation. The enemy you are scared of is not bigger than God who issued this command, so why not hold your peace, and see what He will do. You are too fearful and agitated about many things that don't exist.

When God was issuing this command, He was aware of the battles ahead, but He told them to be still. Think about the Egyptians, the Red Sea, the Anakim, the Jericho wall, the Jordan River, and all the other problems that lay

how to see God's peace at work in your life

ahead of Israel; yet God told them to be still. God knows what is ahead of you. He is aware of all that you are trying to solve with your mind. Certainly there can never be any mountain, wall, or storm too big for God to handle. Only be still, and you will see his ever-present salvation. He is our very present help in times of trouble. He knows the battles ahead and is ever ready to fight for you.

Shortly after this command from the Lord, the children of Israel came face-to-face with the Red Sea with the Egyptians pursuing them from behind. It was one moment that God wanted to test their obedience to the principle of being still. They were scared of the Egyptians who were pursuing them from behind than trusting the Lord God who was leading them. They forgot about this scripture in Exodus 14:13-14, cried, and blamed Moses for the trouble. Such behavior is very common with Christians of our day who throw all their Bible verses away in the face of affliction and hang onto the problem. We tend to magnify the problem instead of our God.

Why do you think God commanded the children of Israel to be quiet while marching around the wall of Jericho? It was because He did not want anybody to magnify the big nature of the wall instead of Him. He needed a serene atmosphere in order to be exalted. When that environment was created, He broke down the mighty walls of Jericho. Later, Moses testified about God saying:

The lord is a man of war: the lord is his name. Who is like unto thee lord, among the gods? Who is like unto thee, glorious in holiness, fearful in praises, doing wonders.

Exodus 15:3, 11

The Lord is moved to fight our battles when we are still in our moments of trouble. He proves to the heathen his wonders. He makes all see and know that there is no other God like Him by His act of intervention. The peace of God also sets the pace for a divine whisper, and illumination in God's word.

how to see God's peace at work in your life

PEACE FOR DIVINE WHISPER AND ILLUMINATION

Peace is a pacesetter for a divine whisper and illumination. You need peace in order to hear the small still voice of God. You need it for a divine whisper on the *rhema* Word of God. The altar of peace must be in place for the Lord to speak to you on any situation. God is not the author of confusion, and so cannot be found in environments with confusion. Remember how God related with Adam and Eve in the Garden of Eden. They heard Him in the cool of the day.

> And they heard the voice of the Lord God walking in the Garden in the cool of the day.
>
> Genesis 3:8

The cool of the day is the time of a serene environment. It's one of the most peaceful moments of the day. It was at that time that Adam and Eve heard the voice of the almighty God in the Garden. Therefore, a peaceful environment can bring down God speaking to us with an audible or still voice.

There are many in the body of Christ today who are fasting and praying to hear a word from the Lord, when the altar of peace is not set right in their lives. Friend, God speaks , but not *to* people in a globe of confusion. The confusion around a man could hinder him from hearing the small, still voice of God. Anytime a cool time is set aside for God, He whispers to us, and gives us a divine illumination into His Word. If you need to hear God's whisper, then you must get into the cave.

Get into the Cave

There are times we get into very difficult issues that we do not know the next step to take in life. We get confused, and all we need in those moments is God's voice for direction and insight. To some, such moments are the times to run around to all their friends for consultations. To others, it is the time to run from one prophet to the other for the word of the Lord. Only a few however, remember to run to God in prayer. I have, on several occasions, come to those moments in life, and all I did was get into the cave.

The cave is the place where a man is totally disconnected from other men to be one-on-one with the Lord in prayer. I refer to the cave as that place where it's only you and God in a serene environment and all you desire is a whisper from heaven. That quiet whisper we desire from the Lord in our moments of anxiety will come when we get into the cave.

I noticed that prophets like Elijah, Elisha, etc., always heard from God more clearly because they were always found in *caves*. They lived on mountains separate from other people. No wonder the Word of God was that near to them. In their day, any time they spoke, the Word of God from their lips came with much accuracy and fulfillment. Elijah got into the cave in his moment of uncertainty.

> And he came thither unto a cave, and lodged there; and, behold, the word of the lord came to him, and he said unto him, what doest thou here.
>
> 1 Kings 19:9

At one time in Elijah's life, he was in distress and wished he was dead (1 Kings 19:1-8). The Bible records that he fell asleep in that distressful moments. And as soon as he slept, an angel came to minister to him. You will notice that the word of the Lord did not come to him throughout all these stages of events. However, the Lord spoke when he

55

lodged in the cave. Consider the word behold, and notice how swift the word of God came as soon he got into the cave. In the same way, God wants to speak to you, but he needs you in the cave. He needs your attention. And as soon as He gets it, He will give you attention.

Sometimes, we are so overshadowed by winds, earthquakes, fires, and the cares of life that it becomes hard for God to get our attention. Get out from there into the cave, and you will hear His still voice.

> And the Lord said, Go forth, and stand upon the mount before the lord. And, behold, the lord passed by, and a great and strong wind rent the mountains, and brake in pieces the rocks before the Lord, but the lord was not in the wind: and after the wind an earthquake; but the lord was not in the earthquake: And after the earthquake a fire; but the lord was not in the fire: and after the fire a small still voice. And it was so, when Elijah heard of it, that he wrapped his face in his mantle, and went out, and stood in the entering of the cave. And behold, there came a voice unto him, and said, what doest thou here, Elijah?
>
> 1 Kings 19:11-13

Watch how Elijah got out of the winds, earthquakes, and fire and entered the cave. He knew that the small, still voice of God is not found in confusion, but in the cave.

The scripture above says that Elijah did not hear the still voice of God in the winds, earthquakes, or in the fire, but in the cave. He needs you out of the winds so that He can speak to you.

I know people who expected God to speak when they were in the earthquakes, fires, and storms of their lives but got no word from Him. You will not hear His whisper from there, so stop wasting your time crying for Him from there. Get out into the cave, and you will hear Him vividly.

Reading the above scripture carefully, you will notice that Elijah first moved out of the storms, earthquakes, and fires, and then later to the cave. He knew what many do not know today. He knew the small, still voice of the Lord cannot be heard in those earthquakes, fires, and storms.

I listened to the testimony of one of the great men of God of our day. He narrated how he was so busy with secular job to the extent that God could not get his attention. He wasn't a pastor then, but God had a big plan of a worldwide ministry for him. All God wanted to do was speak to him in the *cave*.

One day, after a visit to a friend, he was about to get into his car when the Lord whispered to him to make some quiet time with Him in prayer. He disengaged himself from family, friends, work, and even church to spend some time with the Lord. And you will not believe that as soon as he got into the *cave* and started praying, the God of heaven met him right away in a vision. The encounter was

how to see God's peace at work in your life

so mighty that it turned his entire life round. Through that visitation, the Lord spelled out His plan of a worldwide ministry for him. Today, many lives are blessed all over the world through him. Praise the Lord for his life.

One time, Jacob went into the cave. We are told in the Bible that he disengaged from his family and everything to be in prayer (Gen.32:22-24), and the Lord visited him. That visitation eventually led to a change of his name from Jacob to Israel and his status from the deceiver to the prince.

> Then Jacob was left alone, and a Man wrestled with him until the breaking of day. And He said, 'Let Me go, for the day breaks'. But he said 'I will not let you go unless you bless me! So, He said to him, 'What is your name? He said 'Jacob'. And He said Your name shall no longer be called Jacob, but Israel, for you have struggled with God and men and have prevailed.
>
> Genesis 32:24, 26, 27

Staying alone in the Lord's presence creates a way for a divine whisper, and a moment for God to get your attention. It creates a moment for a divine encounter with the Lord.

Friend, there are times God will not be able to show you or speak to you about some things, until you get into the *cave*. Another way to hear a divine whisper is being quiet.

BEING QUIET

There are believers who cannot be quiet for just thirty minutes, and yet want to hear a divine whisper. They are like parrots talking from morning to evening and never getting tired. When such believers encounter any problem, it's time for the whole world to hear them. They cannot hold themselves for just a second. They cannot stop talking and be quiet before God on any issue. Talking wears your spirit and distracts your connection to the small, still voice of God. Stop the talking, and be quiet before God in prayer and meditation, and you will hear His whisper. Personally, anytime I need a whisper from the Lord on some issues, I go before him in quietness. The prophet Isaiah knew the power of quietness. He knew that it creates pace for a divine whisper.

> For thus said the lord God, the Holy One of Israel; in returning and rest shall ye be saved; in quietness and confidence shall be your strength: and ye would not. And thine ears shall hear a word behind thee, saying. This is the way, walk ye in it, when ye turn to the right hand, and when ye turn to the left.
>
> Isaiah 30:15, 21

how to see God's peace at work in your life

Quietness is the secret to a divine whisper. Going to God in quietness and in confidence is where our strength is. Our strength is not in much talking. You are not hearing the still voice of God, because you are always talking about things that don't matter. How can two people be involved in talking at the same time? Who will listen to the other?

There are people who are always praying and not attentive to the voice of the Spirit. We ought to be attentive to hear His voice during prayer; otherwise it becomes a mere talk instead of prayer. Prayer is a two-way communication. You have done your part, so allow God to do His. There are times you just have to be quiet before God, and also listen to Him. Why do the talking all alone? Beware that God wants to be listened to.

In Habakkuk 2:1-2, the prophet Habakkuk narrates his own experience with God:

> I will stand upon my watch, and set me upon the tower, and will watch to see what he will say unto me, and what I shall answer when I am reproved.
> And the Lord answered me, and said...

Quietness in God has ushered people into great destinies, breakthroughs and miracles and I believe that as you obey God through this book, you will wallow in his wonders.

PEACE FOR PROSPERITY

The peace of God is the pacesetter for true prosperity. So, anytime peace reigns in our life, God steps in with His prosperity. Peace goes with prosperity, and I am not surprised that God prospered King Solomon in his day. Remember, his name connotes peace, and he was the only king of Israel who enjoyed so much prosperity in his day.

By the time you are thinking of true prosperity in your life, you must first consider getting yourself acquainted with the peace of God. Job was the wealthiest man in his day. He prospered so much that the devil envied his wealth and accused him before God.

When Job had to give an account of his prosperity, he admitted that in order to walk into that realm of prosperity, you need to rest in His peace.

> Acquaint now thyself with him (God), and be at peace, thereby good shall come unto thee...Then shall thou lay up Gold as the dust and the gold of O-phir as the stones of the break.
>
> Job 22:21, 24

Your acquaintance with God is not enough; you need to be at peace with Him. It is His peace that ushers you into His goodness and prosperity. He does not withhold anything good from them that love Him and walk in His peace.

Job knew the place of peace in prosperity, and no wonder he was the financial champion of his day. He was the wealthiest man in the whole of the East.

David points out the connection of peace and prosperity through the word of God.

> He maketh peace in thy borders, and filleth thee with the finest of the wheat.
>
> Psalm 147:14

Peace around your borders is what attracts the blessings of God into your house. Allow peace around your dwellings, and God's finest wheat (rich, material blessings) will be your portion.

Solomon prospered above any other king in Israel because he set peace round his borders. The Bible records

how to see God's peace at work in your life

that no king before or after Solomon prospered so much like him.

Children of God should beware that if we really want to walk into a realm of true prosperity, we must kick confusion out of every area of our life. Peace is a blessing that God gives to His children for true prosperity.

PEACE IS A BLESSING

The Bible makes it clear that the blessing of God makes us rich and adds no sorrow. If we must tap into God's riches, then we need His blessings. It is His blessings that connect us to His riches and cancels all the sorrows in our lives.

Peace is one of God's blessings for His children, and once it is settled in a man's life, God steps in with sorrow-free riches:

> The Lord will give strength unto his people. The Lord will bless his people with peace.
>
> Psalm 29:11

The peace of God is our strength and blessing. We need it to set the pace for divine prosperity.

how to see God's peace at work in your life

Peace and Giving

Giving must be done with joy. Doing it with joy draws the attention of the Lord to you. The act of giving to the Lord with joy brings His blessings and pushes you up in the financial ladder. Giving without any joy does not bring His blessings. It ends only in frustrations. We are in days where giving is preached all over the church as the channel of prosperity and little said about doing it cheerfully:

> Every man according as he purposeth in his heart, so let him give, not grudgingly, or of necessity: for God loves a cheerful giver.
>
> 2 Corinthians 9:7

Think about it! Giving should not be done out of force. It should be done cheerfully according to our ability. That way we can attract the blessings of God.

How to Walk
in the Peace of God

Inviting Jesus into Your Life

We need Jesus in our lives in order to walk in the peace of God. He said:

> But seek first the kingdom of God and His righteousness, and all these things shall be added to you. Therefore do not worry about tomorrow, for tomorrow will worry about its own things. Sufficient for the day is its own trouble.

> Matthew 6:33-34

The reason why many people can't find the God-kind of peace is because they have rejected Jesus. They have rejected righteousness. They are neither prepared to listen to God nor to have anything to do with Him. They are trying to get peace from worldly goods. Money without God amounts to nothing but disaster. A good job without Jesus will not give you any peace. Jesus has offered us God and righteousness with all the good things of this world as a bonus. Unfortunately, many people are seeking for the bonus instead of the offer, and this is where the missing link is. We cannot break spiritual protocol, so let's do the right thing, and we will enjoy peace with all the wonders connected to it. The right thing is to accept Jesus as our Lord and personal savior, and He will give us the gift of peace.

> Peace I leave with you, My peace I give to you; not as the world do I give to you. Let not your heart be troubled, neither let it be afraid.
>
> John 14:27

He is the prince of peace, and peace is one of the legacies that He has given to His children. Therefore, when we invite Him into our lives through prayer, He will bless us with this gift of peace.

Having a Steadfast Mind on God

In order to walk in the peace of God, you need to have your mind fixed on God. That means that your song about God should always be the same, whether in season or out of season, in tough times, and in good times. You don't sing a song of goodness and shout praise when all is good and then turn around to sing a bad song when things don't go as good as you wish. You can't enjoy His peace with such a flip-flop type of attitude. Have a fixed mind about God. Trust Him even when your faith fails. Remember, trust begins where faith ends.

> You will keep him in perfect peace, whose mind is stayed on You, Because he trusts in You.
>
> Isaiah 26:3

To have your mind stayed on God, is to think about Him often. That means to remember that He is in absolute control over the events of our life. By doing this, we will not be despair over the turn of events in the world. We need to know that he that comes to God must believe that He is, and that He is a rewarder of those who diligently seek Him.

Put your trust in God, and know that He is everything. He is able to do anything. Have your mind fixed on His promises. God is not a man that He should lie or repent

how to see God's peace at work in your life

concerning His promises. David is one man whose mind was stayed or steadfast on God. He walked in peace and enjoyed many wonders in God. He declares:

> Surely he will never be shaken; The righteous will be in everlasting remembrance. He will not be afraid of evil tidings; His heart is steadfast, trusting in the Lord.
>
> Psalm 112:6-7

The key to walking in the peace of God is to have your heart steadfast, trusting in the Lord. You need to stand firm and not be shaken by evil tidings. It does not matter the nature of the evil tidings, all you are required to do is to have your mind stayed on God, and His promises. Your confessions should be positive and based on God's word even when others around you are confessing negative. You must not join the world to sing their songs no matter whatever happens.

God bless you with His peace, and enjoy all the wonders connected to it. Amen! Amen!